UK TAX GUIDE 2018

ESSENTIAL READING FOR EMPLOYED, SELF EMPLOYED AND BUSINESS OWNER

SMART TAX SAVING TACTICS

Copyright © 2018

ITM ANALYSIS

INTRODUCTION

5.5 million* people in the UK are paying more income tax than they should. Many are unknowingly missing out on allowances and deductions they can claim and save hundreds and thousands of pounds every year.

Around 2.5 million are paying less tax so it is important to check and make sure you don't end up receiving a notice from HMRC for a large outstanding payment.

This reference guide is essential reading for all PAYE taxpayers, self-employed and small business owners including limited companies, sole traders and partnerships. It will help you easily navigate through the seemingly complex process of completing you tax return, and claim for allowances and benefits to increase your savings.

The guide will help you check if you qualify for a tax refund, how to claim for it, and how to apply for a tax relief. You can still claim back for previous four years.

*Source: Gov.UK, Policy paper, Helping customers pay the right amount of tax on time, April 2017

TABLE OF CONTENTS

QUICK NOTE ON HOW TO USE THIS GUIDE

Read this guide and if you believe you have overpaid in taxes, or are eligible for an allowance - claim back your money using the helpful links provided in this guide and/or by choosing the correct form on the HMRC website.

You can also pay a reasonable fee and use services of a company such as Taxback (taxback.co.uk) who are government registered agents. They also have an online tool you can use to check if you qualify for a tax refund.

WHY YOU MIGHT BE ENTITLED FOR A TAX REFUND

- ➤ **5.5 million** people in the UK are paying more income tax than they should.

- ➤ **1 in 6** of us is possibly entitled for a tax refund considering approx. 30.1 million pay income tax in the UK.

- ➤ Nearly **50%** of those overpaying belong to the lowest income group. Higher rate tax payers (40% and 50% tax bracket) are also missing out by not claiming for some of the tax reliefs.

- ➤ Almost every expense that you can justify as related to your business will allow for some deductions but thousands are unknowingly missing out by not claiming.

- ➤ **2 million** in the UK are eligible for marriage allowance but do not claim for it. Most of them are simply not aware of this benefit despite HMRC's marketing efforts.

- ➤ Since April 2016, you don't have to declare any income up to the first **£5,000** you receive in dividend payments for shares you own in a company.

New Changes for Tax Year 2018/19

UK Income Tax Rates*

- Personal allowance will increase to £11,850
- Basic tax rate of 20% on additional income of up to £34,500
- Higher 40% tax rate on earnings over £46,350 to £150,000
- Top 45% tax rate on earnings above £150,000
- Capital gains tax will be exempt up to £11,700 (individuals) and £5,850 (trusts)

Scottish Income Tax Rates*

- Personal allowance will increase to £11,850
- Starter tax rate of 19% on additional income of up to £2,000
- Basic tax rate of 20% on earnings from £2,001- £12, 150
- Intermediate tax rate of 21% on earnings from £12,151 to £32,423
- High tax rate of 41% on earnings from £32,424 to £150,000
- Top 46% tax rate on earnings above £150,000

*Source: Gov.UK

Simple Assessment has been introduced

HMRC has introduced this new system to make it easier for many of the estimated 11 million people who file their own tax returns. HMRC can now make better use of the data it has on many of these tax-payers and will be using it to make it easier for such individuals to pay tax without having to complete a tax return – starting for the tax years 2016 and 2017.

For more details, visit Gov.uk and read the Policy paper "Simple Assessment – ending the tax return", 22 September, 2017.

Making Tax Digital System will come into effect April 2019

Start preparing as this will come into effect from April 2019, although initially to declare VAT obligations and only mandatory for businesses that have a turnover over the VAT threshold.

National Minimum Wage and National Living Wage rates*

Worker Age/Category	From April 2017	From April 2018 onwards
25 yrs and above (national living wage rate)	£7.50	£7.83
21 yrs to 24 yrs inclusive	£7.05	£7.38
18 yrs to 20 yrs inclusive	£5.60	£5.90
Under 18 yrs (but above compulsory school leaving age)	£4.05	£4.20
Apprentices under 19 yrs	£3.50	£3.70
Apprentices 19 yrs and over, but in the first year of their apprenticeship	£3.50	£3.70

*Source: Gov.UK

THE BIG ALLOWANCES AND BENEFITS:
HAVE YOU MISSED OUT ON ANY OF THESE?

HIGHER-RATE TAXPAYER: CLAIM ADDITIONAL 20%-25% RELIEF ON YOUR PENSION

Many thousands of high and top rate UK tax payers are not claiming the full relief on their pension contributions. They are losing hundreds and thousands of pounds every year and only getting 20% basic rate tax "Relief at source" that the pension companies add.

If you pay 40% income tax, you are entitled to another 20% tax relief on your pension contributions, and 25% relief if you pay 45% income tax.

The pension tax relief calculator from Prudential (Pru.co.uk) will give you a quick estimate on how much relief you can get.

Take Action

You can claim by your self-assessment tax return.

Higher-rate taxpayers are not claiming back all of their tax relief mistakenly believing they receive it automatically. Read more details at Gov.uk, search for "Tax on your private pension contributions".

You can still revise your tax return for one year, If you did not make this claim. Also, you can claim "overpayment relief" by writing to HMRC within four years.

MARRIAGE ALLOWANCE: CLAIM BACK UP TO £662, IF YOU QUALIFY

Nearly 2 million people in the UK are eligible but have not claimed for this allowance yet. Most are simply not aware of this benefit despite HMRC's increased marketing efforts.

If your partner (married or civil partnership) is not working or earning less than the personal allowance (£11,500 in tax year 2017/18), he/she can transfer up to £1,150 of their allowance to you – provided you are earning between £11,501-£45,000 (£43,000 in Scotland) and pay tax.

Once you start claiming, the allowance will renew by itself every year until your circumstances change, or you decide to stop claiming.

Take Action

For more details and to apply for this claim, visit Gov.uk/apply-marriage-allowance

The annual rebate is £230 but applicants can back date their claim to April 5, 2015. It applies to all, regardless if you have to fill a tax return or not.

MAKE THE BEST USE OF YOUR SPOUSE'S PERSONAL ALLOWANCE

If you are married, or are in a civil partnership – and your partner is not-working/earning less that the personal tax allowance, you can shift your savings and investments e.g. income from a buy-to-let property to your partner, and save tax. This way couples can give each other up to £11,700 a year (2018/19) and avoid capital gains tax.

Further, note that if your net income for 2017/18 is greater than £100K, your personal allowance (£11,500) will reduce by £1 for every £2 of income over £100K. By making more pension contributions and transferring other income generating savings/investments to your partner will help in reducing your tax.

Take Action

Transfer your rental income, returns from your savings and other investments, in your partner's name if they are in the lower tax band (£33,500 for 2017/18).

MAKE FULL USE OF THE MILEAGE ALLOWANCE

Is your mileage allowance less per mile than the permitted rate?

If you are being paid less than 45p a mile for using a car/van for work or business, you can claim the difference for the first 10,000 miles travelled. Above 10,000 miles you can claim 25p per mile.

There is higher tax on company cars so usually the better option is to use your own car/van and claim for permissible mileage using HMRC authorised mileage rates. This is most recommended if your business is setup as a limited company.

Take Action

Find how much you can claim by using the Work Mileage Tax Rebate website.
Workmileagetaxrebate.co.uk

KEEP DIVIDEND PAYMENTS OF £5,000 TAX FREE

Since April 2016, you don't have to declare any income up to the first £5,000 you receive in dividend payments for shares you own in a company.

There's no tax to pay on dividends from shares you own in an ISA.

Share trading involves risks but can offer an attractive tax free income if you can pick your investment wisely.

Take Action

Dividend payments of up to £5,000 you receive is tax free - above that needs to be declared and paid tax on at 7.5% for basic-rate taxpayers and 32.5% for higher rate tax-payers.

Visit Gov.uk and read the policy paper "Dividend Allowance factsheet" to understand how tax applies on dividend payments above the allowance.

NO TAX TO PAY ON SAVINGS INCOME OF £1,000

With your Personal Savings Allowance, up to £1,000 of interest you earn from savings is tax-free if you happen to be a basic-rate taxpayer, and up to £500 if you are a higher-rate taxpayer.

Higher-rate taxpayers can also invest in tax free ISAs (either cash or shares) of up to £15,240 each year.

BENEFIT FROM ADDITIONAL £2,000 FOR YOUR CHILDCARE COSTS

The Tax-Free Childcare scheme was introduced in April 2017 and is being gradually rolled out. It aims to reduce the childcare costs for working parents by another £2,000 per child (£4,000 for a disabled child).

Additionally, since September 2017, parents of 3-4 years old can apply for 30 hours of free childcare, double that of the 15 hours that was available previously.

Take Action

Better childcare offers are available now with the new Childcare Choices government website Childcarechoices.gov.uk

If you have young children, it's worth registering on the website and use the childcare calculator for offers most suitable for you.

MAKE £7,500 TAX FREE FROM RENT-A-ROOM SCHEME

You can earn up to £7,500 (income minus costs) under the rent-a-room scheme using Airbnb, VRBO/HomeAway, etc., without having to declare and pay tax.

This applies only if you are renting out a furnished accommodation, and if you as the landlord live in the same property. For example, if you let out a room in your own house, provide bed and breakfast accommodation, or offer short term lettings such as on Airbnb.

More information is available in the "Rent-a-Room Scheme: HS223 Self-Assessment helpsheet" at Gov.uk, should you be Interested in generating additional income this way.

Tax Saving Tactics for Self-employed and Business Owners

DEDUCT ALL REASONABLE COSTS IF YOU WORK FROM HOME

If you work from home (whether homeowner or renting), you are entitled to deduct all costs that can be attributed in reasonable proportion to the time/space used in your house for work. This can include expenses you incur on heating, lighting, water, home insurance, mortgage interest, council tax, cleaning and maintenance. Expenses for both private and business use e.g. rent, broadband charges, etc. do not qualify for deduction.

For example, if you use one of the three rooms in your house for work then you can justify a third of the house bills and expenses for your work/business. Best practice is to keep the proportion 5%-10% lower i.e. 25%-30% of bills/expenses attributed to work will be good in this case.

Take Action

At the very minimum, you can deduct £4/week (£18/month) which HMRC allows without the need for providing any evidence.

That alone means 52 weeks x £4 = £208 of annual savings, and you can always claim more if you can justify higher actual costs.

CLAIM FOR ITEMS YOU USE IN YOUR BUSINESS

If you are running your business as a sole trader/in-partnership, it is possible to claim for items you use in your business e.g. printer, laptop, desk, chair, etc., even if they were purchased before you started trading.

As per the capital allowance scheme, you can claim 100% allowance for as much as the first £200,000 you spend on buying business/capital items. In case you are planning to spend a considerable amount on such items e.g. plant, machinery, etc., buying it before the tax year ends (April 5) will allow you to claim/deduct the amount you spend against the profit for that year.

Take Action

Check the benefits and pros/cons of operating as a sole trader vs. limited company.

Find the items you can claim for as capital allowances on Gov.uk

FIGURE OUT THE MOST TAX EFFICIENT SALARY FOR YOURSELF AND YOUR PARTNER

If possible, consider taking a salary up to your personal allowance, and what you earn above from your business as dividends. This way you can reduce your tax and NI (National Insurance) contributions if your business is setup as a limited company.

It might be beneficial to pay some amount as salary to your spouse/partner for their work/help on your business. How much you should pay depends on the amount of help and assistance you get, and you should also factor in the other income of your spouse/partner to decide what works best for tax savings. You can also make pension contributions for your spouse/partner or other family members that work in your business.

ENJOY YOUR BUSINESS TRAVEL ALLOWANCE

When travelling for business purposes, make it a comfortable and enjoyable trip. Use a taxi to travel and have meals at good restaurants as deductions for such travel and subsistence costs are fully allowable.

Be reasonable but you don't need to go super cheap on business trips. Consider it one of your deserving perks for which the government is sharing the costs.

SAVE TAX WHILE PROVIDING MEALS FOR YOUR EMPLOYEES

Consider providing free or subsidised meals to your employees, or give vouchers covering the cost of their meals. This way you can reduce your tax and NI on the expense incurred.

Enjoy a nice dinner, or a well-deserved annual party or two with your spouse/partner and other friends and family members that work/assist you in your business. The expense is tax deductible – just keep the annual expense per person for such parties and meals under £150 and only claim for those who do some work to help grow your business.

Take Action

For more details on what you can claim as meals for employees and directors, read the page "Expenses and benefits: meals for employees and directors" on Gov.uk

OTHER TACTICS TO REDUCE YOUR TAXES

Pay for childcare costs for any people you employ using a salary sacrifice scheme. In most cases (check full details and restrictions on Gov.uk) childcare voucher schemes are tax-free for employee, and as employer you won't have to pay National Insurance.

Have your mobile service plan in the name of your business and this way you can easily have all the business related phone costs tax deductible. This could save you up to £500 a year on a high-end smartphone with a generous voice/data plan.

OTHER BENEFITS
YOU ARE ENTITLED TO

CLAIM BACK ON YOUR CHARITABLE DONATIONS

Higher-rate taxpayers who have made gift-aided donations to charities can claim back on the higher-rate tax they have paid.

For example, if you donate £5 every month to your favourite charity, the total annual value of your gift-aided donation will be (5 X 12 X 1.25 = £75) and you can claim back £15 if you pay tax at 40%.

Tax relief on these donations include membership to the National Trust and entry fee to most zoos. National Trust membership allows free entry 500+ special places, and free parking at most of their car parks. The family membership (currently £114.60 a year) will provide a tax rebate of £28.65 for higher-rate taxpayers, if it is gift aided.

GET TAX REBATE FOR ANY PROFESSIONAL/UNION FEES YOU PAY

If your work/profession involves registration to, or a licence from, a professional body or a union - you can claim tax rebate on the fees you pay.

HM Revenue & Customs has a list of approved bodies that fall in this category and you can deduct their fees from your income before tax.

Go to Gov.uk and look for "Approved professional organisations and learned societies", 19 January, 2018.

As an example, The National Union of Teachers (standard annual subscription for £179) is on the list of approved bodies.

You can get this tax relief if you subscribe to a body or a union you believe is beneficial, even if it is not mandatory for your work/profession.

DEDUCT £80-£140 FOR UNIFORM COSTS

HMRC now allows flat-rate reductions of up to £140 a year for people doing business or work that requires wearing a uniform. This includes protective clothing, and costumes for entertainers and actors.

You might still be able to claim a standard annual sum of £60 in tax relief even if your occupation is not listed so it may be worth asking for.

Take Action

More details and the qualifying list of occupation can be found at Gov.uk under "Employment Income Manual".

SMART TIPS

AND

BEST PRACTICES

CHECK IF YOU CAN REDUCE TAX BY CHANGING YOUR BUSINESS SETUP

The taxes you have to pay can significantly vary depending on your business structure. Check whether it's better to run your business as a sole trader, in-partnership, or whether you can save more by setting up a limited company.

Take Action

Check the benefits and pros/cons of operating as a sole trader vs. limited company. A good summary can be found at SimplyBusiness.co.uk – Look for the article titled "What's the difference between a sole trader and a limited company?"

Maintain a separate bank account and credit card for your business

This will save you hours of work and make it a lot easier to accurately calculate your business expenses, enabling you to quickly complete your Self-Assessment and submit your tax return.

Take Action

Use different folders/files to keep all the documents sorted throughout the year. Maintain separate folders for sales orders, expense receipts, ATM withdrawals, bills, etc. Keep a couple of hours every month to make sure you are keeping the folders updated

BORROW FOR BUSINESS, AVOID PERSONAL LOANS

Manage your personal and business bank accounts in a way that interest payments for any loans and borrowings on your personal account are minimum. It's better to have majority of the interest payments for loans or overdraws on your business account as they are deductible for tax.

Take Action

The smart practice is to keep transactions between your business and personal accounts to minimum throughout the year. Especially, avoid any funding of your business account by overdrawing on your personal accounts, or with personal loans and borrowings.

USE A RELIABLE TAX SOFTWARE FOR ACCURATE SELF-ASSESSMENT

Every year thousands are fined by HMRC for not completing and/or submitting incorrect self-assessment.

Consider using an accounting software such as QuickBooks Online so you can easily record your income and expenses throughout the year. Plenty of reasonably priced tax and accounting software and mobile apps are available such as QuickBooks Intuit.

Take Action

Which is offering a service (£10 for members, £30 non-members) in partnership with SimpleTax to calculate and submit tax return to HMRC directly on your behalf. The service is recognised by HMRC and may save you time and avoid mistakes in your self-assessment.

Calculate your tax using the Which Tax Calculator
Which.co.uk/money/tax-calculator

SUBMIT YOUR TAX RETURN ONLINE

Register on HMRC's website for submitting your Self-Assessment online.

The benefit of submitting online is that your tax gets calculated automatically while you fill the tax return, and you receive instant confirmation and reference number for records.

Also, you will receive a faster repayment in case HMRC owes money to you.

MAKE NECESSARY AMENDMENTS, EVEN AFTER THE JAN 31 DEADLINE

Are you aware that you can amend your tax return even after the Jan 31 deadline? Yes, this is possible and although HMRC has the right to charge penalties, they very rarely do so.

It's better to correct a false information even after the deadline and you can do so by just going online to amend your tax return. There's no need to contact HMRC first.

FINAL RECOMMENDATIONS

RECOMMENDATIONS FOR SELF-EMPLOYED AND BUSINESS OWNERS

Call HMRC first to discuss your queries as that often is the quickest and easiest way to resolve any clarifications you need. The service is pretty good and they send you relevant forms and information in post, if necessary.

Register on HMRC's website for submitting your Self-Assessment online, if they ask or advise to do so. This way you will also receive a faster repayment in case HMRC owes money to you.

Be reasonable and imaginative as almost every expense that you can justify as related to your business will allow for some deductions. Therefore, think about other expenses that you can claim for - just make sure you are keeping good records and receipts, especially as for some expenses you may be asked to provide more details or explanation to HMRC.

RECOMMENDATIONS FOR PAYE TAXPAYERS

Make sure your Tax Code is correct

Thousands of salary earners in the UK are paying more tax than they should because of incorrect tax code.

Your tax code reveals your deductions and allowances to calculate your tax. It works with certain assumptions and despite HMRC's efforts to reduce instances of people overpaying/underpaying, the issue is far from being resolved.

Changes in your expenses like taking a new private medical insurance, or giving up the company car will impact how much tax you should/need to be paying. Also, any changes to your partner's income, children you have, etc. can impact on the allowances you may claim for and your taxes.

Take Action

Check that your tax code is correct, understand what the letter/s in your tax code mean and how it impacts your Personal Allowance. Get more details at Gov.uk/tax-codes

You can also use the PAYE Tax Calculator at Listentotaxman.com to check your tax, pension/national insurance contributions, and allowances and deductions, to see if your take home pay matches with your pay-slips.

LEGAL NOTES

ITM Analysis offers a range of practical and easy-to-use guides to help consumers achieve their career, business, and financial goals.

Notice/Disclaimer

www.ingramcontent.com/pod-product-compliance
Lightning Source LLC
Chambersburg PA
CBHW071157220526
45468CB00003B/1062